Mel Bay's
Electric Bass Position Studies

by Roger Filiberto

POSITION STUDIES FOR ELECTRIC BASS IS AN ESSENTIAL SUPPLEMENT TO OUR ELECTRIC BASS METHOD VOLUMES 1 & 2, BY ROGER FILIBERTO. IT IS A VALUABLE COURSE OF STUDY FAMILIARIZING THE BASS PLAYER WITH KEY RELATIONSHIPS ON UP THE NECK.

UPON COMPLETION OF THIS TEXT, THE SERIOUS STUDENT SHOULD MOVE ON TO THE MEL BAY'S DELUXE ENCYCLOPEDIA OF ELECTRIC BASS ARPEGGIOS.

Mel Bay

The meteoric rise in prominence and popularity of the Electric Bass is comparable to the world wide acceptance and popularity of the Electric Guitar.

In its early years, the late '40's, the Electric Bass was limited to the Rock and Roll style. However, within the past decade the Electric Bass has emerged as a "true" musical instrument, reaching to greater heights in sound and performance as never before.

The versatility of the Electric Bass has been instrumental in drawing the attention of musicians and jazz "buffs" of the world as no other instrument since the advent of the Electric Guitar.

There are volumes of fine books that offer many of the new Bass lines and Patterns. However, if you are not yet a knowledgeable musician much of this material is not playable by the average Electric Bassist.

There is **NO** position instruction book for the Electric Bass on the market at the present time, and it is with this thought in mind that this method is being published. The knowledge that you will acquire through the excellent and varied studies presented in this method will enable you to perform all of the exciting new styles offered you in many of the fine publications now on the market.

The Author,

Roger Filiberto

SCALE OF NOTES IN FIFTH POSITION
Ascending In Sharps - Descending In Flats

First Study In Fifth Position

Study No.2

* The 4th finger is recommended for a smoother execution of this figure.

Study No.3

Scale Of C Major In Fifth Position

* Observe optional fingering B to C and back to B at end of 2nd measure and extending into the 3rd measure. Practice both ways.

Study No. 4 In C Major

Study No. 5 In C Major

Study No. 6   A Walk In F Major

MIXED POSITION STUDY
First Position   And Fifth Position
Excellent Study In Shifting

Shifting from the 1st position to the 5th position can be accomplished very quickly and easily with a little dedicated effort and practice.

*Longer Walk In C Major - Fifth Position

Moving It

* "Longer Walk" and "Moving It" should also be practiced in the second position. For a review of 2nd position thru 7th position scales see charts in E. B. Vol. 2 pa. 12-14.

Walk In A Minor
Fifth Position

*Observe unusual but effective fingering in 11th and 12th measures

F Major Waltz - Fifth Position

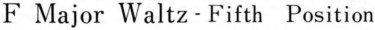

The above study can also be played in 1st position.

Boogie Walk In C Major - Fifth Position

Complete B♭ Major Scale In Fifth Position

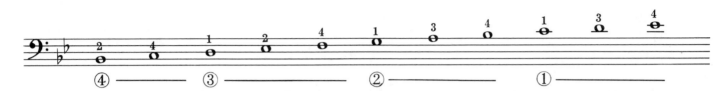

Bright Walk In Fifth Position

Moderately bright

Complete E♭ Major Scale In Fifth Position

Long Walk In E♭

Solid four

16 Bar Walk In D Minor - Fifth Position

* Observe unusual fingering for smoother movement

Etude In 6/8 Time - Fifth Position

12 Bar Boogie In Fifth Position - Key of B♭

"MOUNTAIN PASS"
Fifth Position Study

LES WISE

*Take notice of the unusual fingering in this measure.   The above study should also be practiced
in the 1st position.

STANDARD SHUFFLE PATTERN
Key of B♭ In Fifth Position

𝄎 = Repeat previous measure

TRIPLET STUDY IN D
Second Position Review

Solid Four
Walk In D Minor

Ben marcato

More Of The Same - In B♭

Moderately bright

Greater variety and dimension can be added to any walk style by changing a straight four beat to any of the patterns shown below. But don't over do it. Use occasionally.

"Classical Walk" In Fifth Position

An interesting study in the key of Bb using "neighboring" notes

Observe how the frequent and tasteful use of neighboring notes embellishes the diatonic scale tones and chordal patterns thereby eliminating the "routine" sound of this type of study.

This study should also be practiced in the 1st position. Disregard suggested fingering when practicing in the 1st position.

For variety you may substitute any of the "rhythmic figures" shown below for any measure in the above Classical Walk. Use tastefully and occasionally. These figures create a feeling of real "jazz drive".

SYNCOPATION MADE EASY
Fifth Position

Sections A and B are played and sound exactly alike. In section B tied eighth notes are substituted for the quarter notes in section A.

LONDON "BOOGIE"
Syncopation Study In Fifth Position

After satisfactory progress has been made in the 5th position you may then practice this study in the 2nd position. * See foot-note

* See the Mel Bay Electric Bass Vol. 2, page 38 for the C major scale and chart in the 2nd position.

MODERATO
A Study In Syncopation

Also practice this study in 2nd position, disregarding suggested fingering

* Examples "A" and "B" are played and sound exactly the same. In the fourth measure of section B we substitute two tied eighth notes for the quarter note in section A. In the seventh measure of section B we substitute a tied eighth note to a quarter note in place of the dotted quarter note in section A.

Syncopation

*In the 2nd, 3rd, 4th and 6th measures of Section "B" we substitute tied eighth notes for the quarter notes in section "A".

ALLEGRETTO
A Touch Of Syncopation

* Observe fingering in 5th measure.

Slur Study No. 1

* Descending slur—Sound the 1st note of the "slur" and pull-off or lift off left hand finger from the second note of slur.

** Ascending slur—Sound the 1st note and slide same finger to second note. Can also be played by hammering on the next left hand finger on the second note of slur.

Slur Study No. 2

Observe that in the above studies the "slide slur" is suggested in the ascending passages due to the necessity of remaining in 5th position.

Bugaloo In Fifth Position

* This sign indicates repetition of the previous TWO measures.

** Although the fingering indicated in this and the next measure (9th & 10th measures) breaks the pattern, study as indicated in order to help master the 5th position. Later, when studying the 7th position you may return to this "Bugaloo" and play these two measures with the same pattern as introduced in the 1st two measures.

Mixed Study In First And Fifth Positions

This study can also be played entirely in the 5th position. The suggestion to use the 1st and 5th positions is to give the student practice in shifting.

16

Jumping With Pleyel

Latin Beat-Progressive Style

* Observe slurs.

The Ghost Dances
In D Minor

* Observe fingering———— play as suggested. It will make these passages smoother.

Chromatic Walk

THE SEVENTH POSITION
Table Of Notes In Seventh Position

Pages 18, 19 and 20 will be devoted to the "easy" approach through the use of simple rhythms of standard songs, thus making it possible for you to get the proper and necessary solid foundation which will make the later more difficult works easier to execute.

First Study In Seventh Position

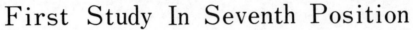

SEVENTH POSITION ETUDE
"In the Mood for a Walk"

* Observe 4 measures of rest.

LATIN FLAVOR
More In Seventh Position

Easy Melody
In Seventh Position

SPANISH BALLAD
An Excellent Study In Seventh And Sixth Positions

* Play the entire E major section in 6th position

Syncopation Study No.1 - Seventh Position

Examples A and B are played and sound the same.

In example B eighth notes, tied, are substituted for the quarter notes in example A.

This study will be of further help in reading SYNCOPATION

Syncopation Study No.2 - Seventh Position

SYNCOPATION study Number two is a bit more complicated than study number one. However, the illustrations are along the same lines. Examples A and B are played and sound the same. In example B tied eighth notes are substituted for the quarter notes in example A. Practice these syncopation studies with sincerity and dedication and you will be well rewarded.

Seventh Position Etude

> The above etude is a tricky 16 bar invention with emphasis on "syncopation".
>
> At this point you can review the second position by practicing this same study in the second position. Observe that the left hand fingering is exactly the same in BOTH positions.

*Seventh Position Etude
Syncopation And "Walk"

* The above etude should also be studied in 1st position

SCALE OF C MAJOR
In The Second And Seventh Position

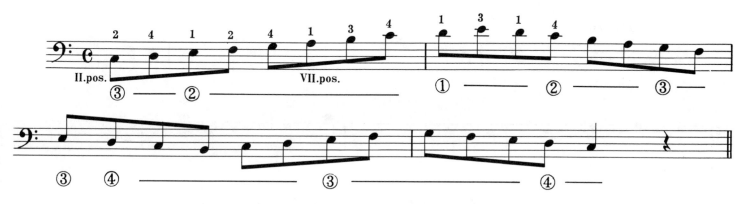

The above study can be played entirely in the 7th position. It is written in the 2nd and 7th positions in order to give you practice in shifting.

Study In Thirds

Play the above study entirely in the 7th position.

WALKING THE C MAJOR SCALE
A Study in Shifting Positions using the 1st, 3rd, 5th, and 7th Position.

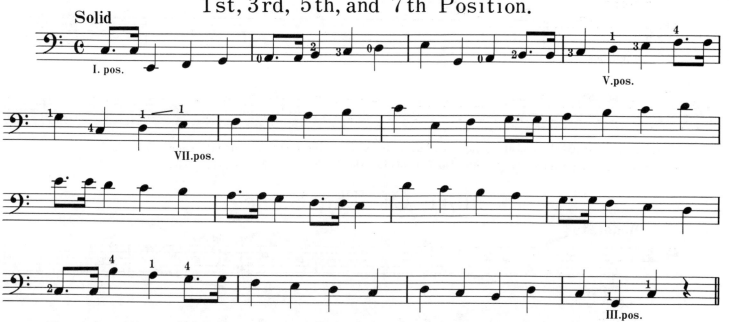

The above study, with diligent practice, will facilitate the shifting of the left hand from one position to another and help develop accuracy.

FOUR SHORT STUDIES IN SEVENTH POS.
Syncopation Study

VII. pos.

＊ = Bend to E♭

More On The Ascending Slur

＊ Strike the grace note G♯ and slide up to principal note A using 1st finger of the left hand for both notes. This is known as the "ascending slur".

More On The Descending Slur

＊ This is the "descending slur". Play the 1st note of the slur (B♭) in the usual manner and "pull off" this note to produce the A note. Do not strike the "A" note with the right hand.

More Of The Same

＊ Ascending slur.

More Syncopation
Fifth And Seventh Positions

* Observe unusual fingering in all measures with the asterisk(*) We recommend this departure from the accepted fingering, and suggest shifting of positions in order to insure smoother performance.

Rockin' In G
Second And Fourth Positions

Rockin' In B♭
Fifth And Seventh Positions

Walking In Fifth And Seventh Positions

Arpeggio Study In Seventh Position

Fifth And Seventh Position Blues

The above is an 8 bar blues pattern using the Tonic, Sub-dominant and dominant chords. (the 1, 4 and 5 chords)
You can transpose this pattern to the key of C by moving it to the 3rd fret and the key of E and playing in
the 7th position. *

FOLK TUNE
Practice In Seventh Pos. Then In Second Pos.

* Obviously this pattern can be transposed to any key by beginning with the
  root of the chord on any fret of the 2nd or the 3rd strings.

D MINOR STUDY
Seventh Position

* Observe unusual fingering in these indicated measures.

A MINOR STUDY
Seventh Position

Stays in its position throughout with no unusual fingering.

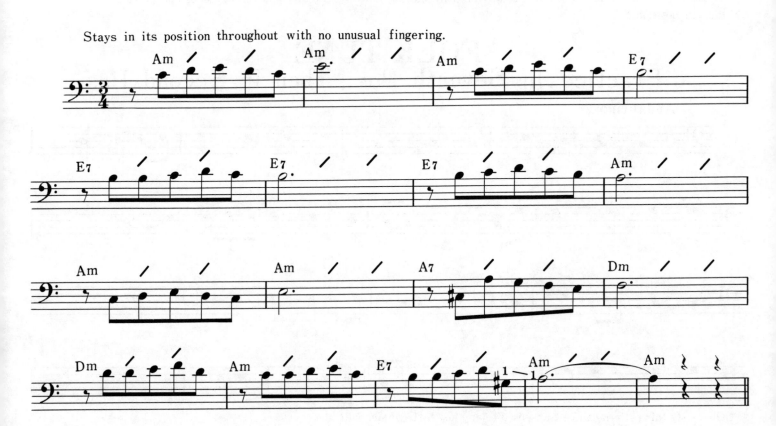

MELODY IN F - Seventh Position
A Study In Syncopation

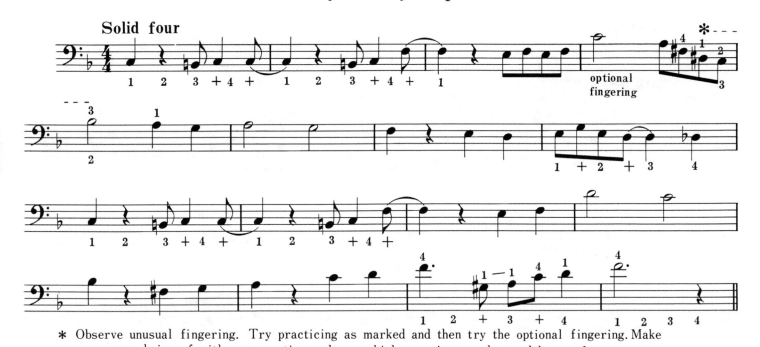

* Observe unusual fingering. Try practicing as marked and then try the optional fingering. Make your own choice of either suggestion and use which ever is smoother and better for you.

FRENCH FOLK SONG
Syncopation In Seventh Position

* Bend to A♭

** Difficult syncopation. See example (capitals) Section B substitutes tied eighth notes for quarter notes in Section A).

SYNCOPATING BACH
Seventh Position

Observe that the left hand fingering is exactly the same in 2nd position as in the 7th position.

✱ Syncopation Aid

No. 1   No. 2   No. 3

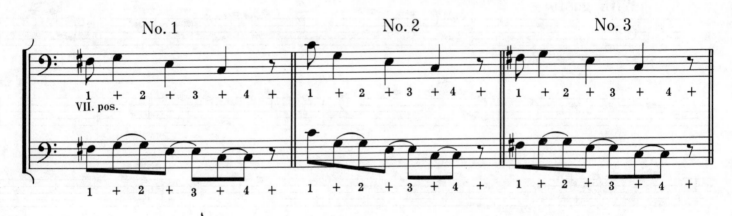

LONDON BRIDGE BOOGIE

Same Syncopation Figures As The "Bach"

"CLASSICAL STUFF"
Seventh Position Study

* Repeat the 1st eight measures in the 2nd position.

C Major Etude - Seventh Position

* When repeating the D.C. al Fine play in the 2nd position. Observe that the fingering is exactly the same as in the 7th position. Make transition smoothly.

MOON WALK
Mixed Position Studies

The above bass part is typical of the style used in popular or progressive music. Root and 5th, scale lines and chord arpeggios dominate this tune which has an abundance of chord changes that move freely, challenging the bassist to make use of the many different positions already presented in the book.

THE NINTH POSITION
Table Of Notes In The Ninth Position

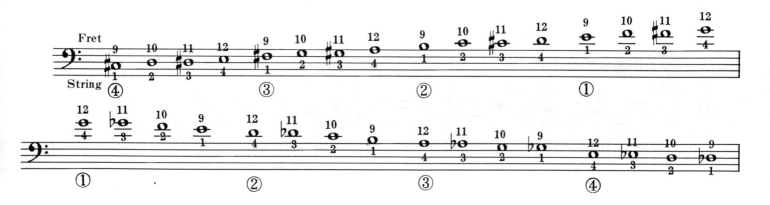

First Study In Ninth Position

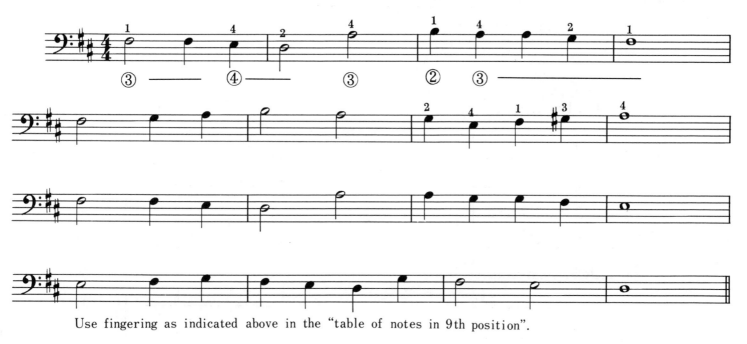

Use fingering as indicated above in the "table of notes in 9th position".

The Scale Of D Major In Ninth Position

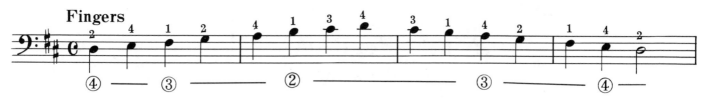

Diatonic Study In D Major - The Ninth Position

The D Major Scale In The Fourth Position
And Ninth Position Are FINGERED ALIKE.

The following examples should be very interesting as well as informative to the serious student.

4th Position
See Diagram No. 1

9th Position
See Diagram ♯2

No.1
4th Position

No.2
9th Position

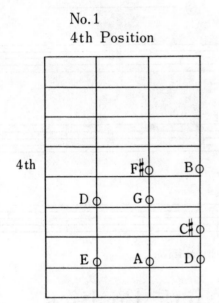

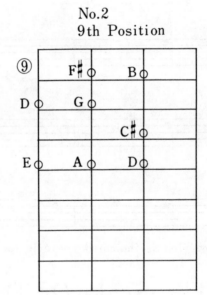

Ninth Position Scale
Containing C♮

The cancellation of the C♯ to a C♮ actually places this scale in the key of G

An Easy Study In Ninth Position
Key Of C Major

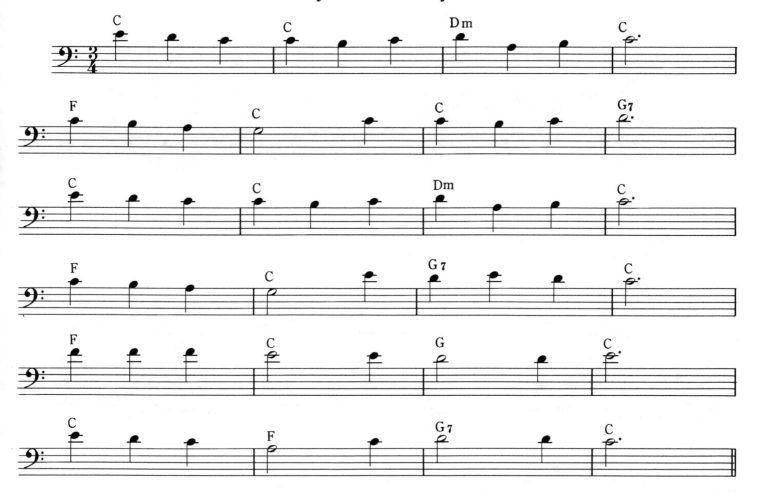

More In The Ninth Position
The Key Of C Major

* Observe unusual fingering in several measures.

STUDY OF THIRDS IN D MAJOR
The Ninth Position

With A Latin Flavor

This study is written in the Ninth Position but moves to the Seventh Position in the Third and Fourth measures.

* Play this measure in the 7th Position.

Eight Bar "Bounce" In The Ninth Position

Take notice of the E♯ in the fourth fret

A WALK IN C MAJOR
Seventh And Ninth Position

This is an excellent study in the traditional "Walk" style and fairly easy in the 7th and 9th positions. You can however, make this study a real challenge by playing the 1st four measures and measures 17 through 20 in the 2nd position.

Diatonic Study In Eighth Notes - Ninth Position

Pay strict attention to the fingering in the 3rd, 4th and 5th measures

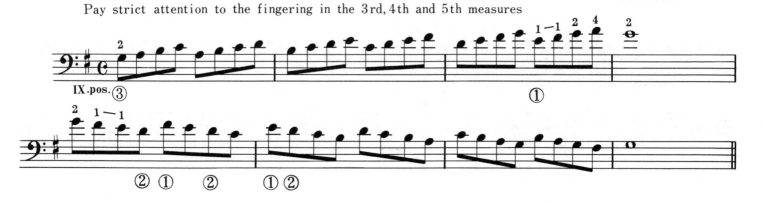

D Major Study In Ninth Position

Solid four

Eight Bars Of Bach - Ninth Position

Minor Mode - Ninth Position

Lively

* Observe unusual fingering.

The A Major Scale, One Octave Only
In The Second And Fourth Positions

II.pos. IV.pos

* At this point you change to the 4th position.   This is an A 6th arpeggio

Riff In Fourth And Fifth Positions

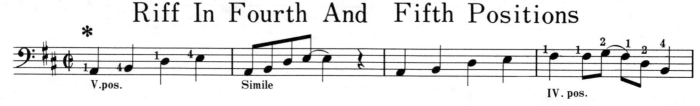

V.pos.   Simile   IV. pos.

* The use of the 4th finger in this passage is optional. You may use the 3rd finger if more comfortable or smoother.

The G Major Scale In Two Octaves
In The Second, Fourth And Ninth Positions
This is an excellent study in shifting and should be practiced ascending and descending.

II.pos. ④ ——— ③ ——————— ② IV.pos——————— ① IX. pos.

Moving It!
A fine Study in Shifting from 2nd to 4th and to 9th position

With drive

II.pos.

IV.pos.   IX.pos.

A Typical Bass Line On A Standard Tune
Key Of E Minor In The Seventh Position

Moderato Can also be played in 2nd position with an occasional move into 1st position.

Pike's Peak

An unusual study involving the 6th, 9th and 11th positions

* When repeating use 1st finger on the "E" note in the 1st measure.

CRAZY QUILT
Multi-Position Study
Using All Positions 2nd Thru 9th

The bass pattern of the three measures 5, 6 and 7 is exactly the same as in measure 13, 14 and 15. There are two different fingering patterns suggested. Both are correct. Fingering is optional. Use whichever is best for you.

Crazy Quilt   Guitar accompaniment

C6 / C#m6 /	G7 // G9	C6 / C#m6 /	G7 // G9	C / E9 /	Eb9 / A7 /	D9 / G9 /	C / / /
C6 / C#m6 /	G7 // G9	C6 / C#m6 /	G7 // G9	C / E9 /	Eb9 / A7 /	D9 / G9 /	C C7 Gm7 C7
F9 / / /	F9 / / /	C ///	C C7 Gm7 C7	F9 / / /	F9 / / /	C / / /	Dm7 / G7 /
C6 / C#m6 /	G7 / G9 /	C6 / C#m6 /	G7 // G9	C / E9 /	Eb9 / A7 /	D9 / G9 /	C / / ‰ ‖

"BREEZY"

An interesting modern jazz style composition for lead guitar with chord accompaniment and an exciting Bass line in several positions including the first position. Fingering is optional and this tune offers the serious student an opportunity to show what he has learned.

An original by
ROGER FILIBERTO

MINOR MOOD
Key Of A Minor -Ninth Position

* Observe the unusual fingering in the 9th and 10th complete measures.
  We suggest this fingering in order to facilitate reaching high "A" , 14th fret, 1st string

** Note the shift to 10th position in this measure for obvious reasons

Ninth Position Study in the Key of D Major

using arpeggios on the three principal chords in this key-The Tonic Chord "D"-(DF♯A) The sub-dominant Chord "G"-(GBD) and the dominant chord "A"-(AC♯E)

2 To 7 Shift (A Review)

A solid Walk study covering the 2nd through 7th Positions.

The above walk study was created to help the student achieve excellence and accuracy in shifting. Follow the suggested fingering strictly and diligently. Positive improvement will be your reward.

We suggest the Mel Bay publication "New Sounds" at this stage for further development of positions.

* The suggested use of the 3rd finger on this "F" note facilitates the movement and use of the 2nd finger on the following "G" note.

Keep Moving

A fine "walk study" in C Major with emphasis in "Shifting" Positions. See foot-note *.

* You will find the above study very useful in developing accuracy in "shifting". Observe the number of different positions employed throughout this study.

In the first measure you have a choice of beginning in either the 2nd or 7th positions. Notice and memorize the association of positions with the guitar chord symbols.

The C Major and C7 arpeggios are generally related to the 2nd or 7th positions., the E Major and E7 arpeggios to the 6th position., the A Major and A7 arpeggios to the 4th position., the D Major and D7 arpeggios to the 4th position., G major and G7 with the 2nd position. The F Major chord or arpeggio can be played in the 2nd position, but because of the high F note at the 10th fret it becomes necessary to use the 7th position.

** This C7 arpeggio could stay in 2nd position but because of the necessity for playing the following F Chord in the 7th position the entire movement becomes much more simple in 7th position. You may try in the 2nd position······you will then become convinced of the choice of 7th position.

Cycle of "fourth's" in all the keys and in all positions from the 1st through 7th positions.
An interesting "walk" study in all of the major chords.

At the student's discretion he may substitute patterns A & B for any walk study

The following study is a variation of the above cycle of fourths. Only the 1st two chords, C & F are shown. You may, however, continue the pattern through all of the keys and all the positions in the previous study.

* Observe the introduction of the "7th" interval.

Still another variation of the above exercises, this one in $\frac{3}{4}$ time. Only the 1st four chords are shown·········continue through all of the keys. Observe that all of the chords in all the studies on this page begin on the root of the chord.

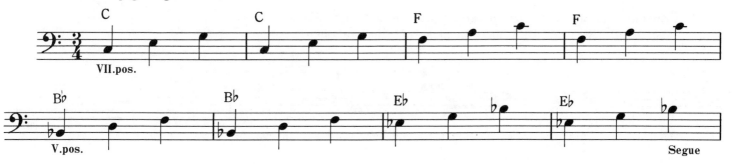

CYCLE OF FOURTHS
Continued from Page 47

Play all of the following studies in the Cycle of Fourths as in previous page. This particular study to be used with <u>Major</u> chords only.

1

The use of dotted 8th notes and 16th notes in the next three studies gives a completely different "feel" to the patterns.   Practice in all keys and positions.

2

3

4

The use of dotted 8th notes and 16th notes throughout this study places it in the "Boogie" classification.

5

Another example of how much variety we can give a straight walk exercise by merely using dotted 8th notes and 16th notes in place of a quarter note.

6

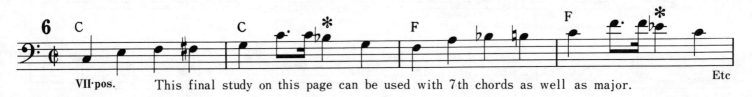

This final study on this page can be used with 7th chords as well as major.

✳ The 7th of the chord.